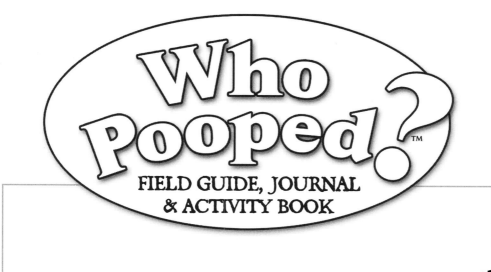

Who Pooped?™

FIELD GUIDE, JOURNAL & ACTIVITY BOOK

D1372643

DRAW OR PLACE A PHOTO OF YOURSELF ABOVE

Name ....

Age .... Date ....

If found contact ....

FLIP BOOK FUN!

This book is not only a field guide, field journal, and activity book, it is also a flip book! Flip books have been around since the 1800s. They make drawings on several pages come to life, moving like a cartoon.

On the edge of every right page in this book, you'll see a little bear cub and a tree. If you flip the pages of the book with your thumb real fast from front to back, you will see the bear climbing up the tree. To make it even more like a cartoon, color the bear and the tree.

On the edge of the left pages, you'll see just a tree. Try drawing your own animal climbing the tree. On every page draw your animal a little higher. Use the bear on the right page as a guide. After you have drawn your animal on every page and it is at the top, flip the pages from the back to the front real fast and watch your animal climb down the tree. Cool!

ISBN: 978-1-56037-726-9

© 2019 by Farcountry Press

Illustration and text by Steph Lehmann

Who Pooped? is a registered trademark of Farcountry Press.

For more information about our books, write Farcountry Press, P.O. Box 5630, Helena, MT 59604;
call (800) 821-3874; or visit www.farcountrypress.com.

 Produced and printed in the United States of America.

MY ADVENTURES

Adventures are AWESOME—filled with excitement and discovery! With this field guide, journal, and activity book, you'll have fun learning about things found in nature, and you'll be able to make a personalized keepsake of your experiences so you'll never forget the fun times you had.

SOME TIPS FOR JOURNALING:

- Get colored pencils, gel pens, or crayons that you love! Keep them in a zippered pouch so you don't lose them. Don't use felt tip pens—they may bleed through to the next page.

- Have tape or a glue stick to add mementos to your journal, like ticket stubs, postcards, notes, drawings, or photos.

- Color everything you can on all the pages. Make every page yours!

- Don't worry about coloring, drawing, and writing perfectly. Just have fun! This is *your* journal. There are no rules!

- Be quiet and pay attention to the natural world around you while on your adventures. You'll be amazed at what you might notice that you haven't before! If you can't journal while in nature, take notes as soon you can, while it's still fresh in your mind.

- If you would like more space for journaling or pictures, tape extra pieces of paper into your journal any place you like. This is called a "tip-in."

TRACK YOUR ADVENTURES

On the map below, color in the states where you've had adventures. If you took a car trip, draw the route you took.

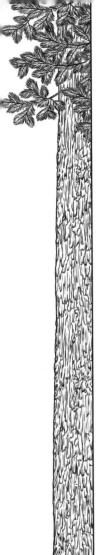

My adventure highlights I always want to remember _____

_____

_____

_____

_____

_____

_____

ADVENTURES LOG: WHERE I WENT AND WHEN

Log your adventures here.

Place

Date

Place

Date

Place

Date

Place

Date

Place

Date

Place

Date

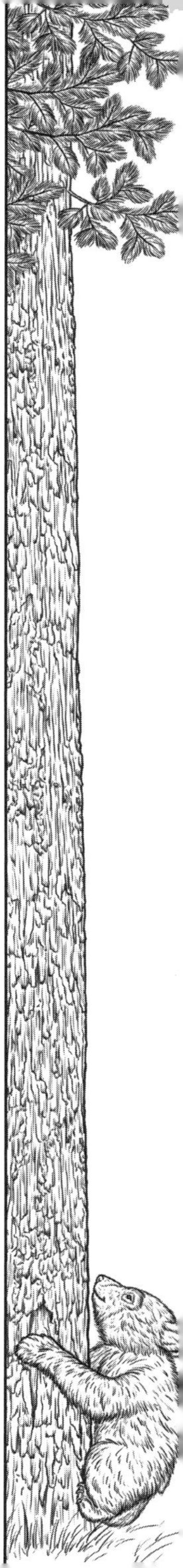

DRAW AND COLOR YOUR
ULTIMATE DAY HIKE PACKING LIST

Comfortable Shoes	Backpack (to carry all your stuff)	Water Bottle (bring extra water)	Snacks (that don't need refrigeration)
Extra Socks	First-Aid Kit	Wet Wipes	Toilet Paper
Camera (if you don't have one on your phone)	Binoculars (cool, but optional)	Bear Spray (when hiking where bears live)	Whistle (in case you get lost or need help)

Flashlight (with extra batteries)	Jacket	Hat	Sunglasses
Sunscreen	Insect Repellent	Map	Cell Phone
Trash bag (to pack out trash)	Towel (to sit on or dry off)	Favorite Toy (for young hikers)	Your *Who Pooped?* *Field Guide/Journal* (with pens or pencils)

MY FAVORITE ADVENTURE TRAIL MIX!

Create your own delicious trail mix recipe to make and take on your adventures.
☑ Check your ingredients and write the name of your trail mix recipe below.

INGREDIENT OPTIONS:

- ❏ 2 cups of your favorite nuts*
- ❏ 2 cups of your favorite cereal
- ❏ 2 cups popped popcorn
- ❏ 2 cups pretzels
- ❏ 2 cups cheese crackers
- ❏ 1 cup chocolate chips or M&Ms
- ❏ 1 cup peanut butter chips
- ❏ 1 cup raisins or other dried fruit
- ❏ 1 cup dried banana chips
- ❏ 1 cup coconut flakes
- ❏ 1 cup mini marshmallows

I also like to add these ingredients:

- ❏ _____
- ❏ _____
- ❏ _____
- ❏ _____

DRAW A PICTURE OF YOUR TRAIL MIX HERE:

DIRECTIONS:

Into a large bowl, add your favorite ingredients from the list above and mix. Place 1 cup trail mix in ziplock baggies for individual servings.

Add nuts only if no one in your group has nut allergies.

SAFE AND RESPONSIBLE OUTDOOR ADVENTURES

Fill in the blanks. (Answers on page 96.)

LEAVE NO TRACE:

- Pack in/pack out: whatever you bring with you must be taken out with you— unless you see a designated _____ to put your trash in.
- Be prepared by always bringing a _____ for your trash, and that includes toilet paper.
- Stay on the trail. Not only is it safer, but then you won't _____ on fragile flowers and small plants. If you do, they may not be able to grow back.
- When in national and state parks, leave what you find for others to enjoy. Do not pick flowers or leaves, or take rocks home. Instead, take photographs or draw _____ of the things you find and want to remember.

KNOW BEFORE YOU GO:

- Plan your trip and research any trails you will be taking. Find out what the _____ will be like so you know how to dress.
- If hiking, always let someone *not* with your group know where you will be going in case your group gets _____ .
- Pack everything you might need on your trip, including items you may need in case of an _____ . *(See Ultimate Packing List on pages 6 and 7.)*

RESPECT WILDLIFE:

- Do not _____ the wildlife.
- Observe them from a distance. Do not try to _____ wild animals.

FIRE:

- Never start a fire without an _____ .
- _____ have fires in designated areas.
- Only use wood found on the _____ . Never snap branches off trees or shrubs.
- Make sure your fire is completely _____ and cold before leaving it.

SAFETY:

- Never hike _____ . Stay within eyesight of an _____ .
- While on a trail, always stop at _____ in the trail to wait for the rest of your group.

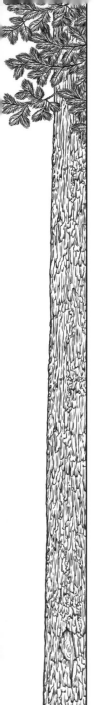

MY ADVENTURES JOURNAL

Today's date _____

Where I was today _____

_____

Who was with me _____

_____

_____

What the weather was like _____

What I ate _____

_____

My favorite things I saw today _____

_____

_____

My favorite things I did today _____

_____

_____

Interesting noises or smells _____

_____

_____

In the box below, draw a picture or place something like a photo, postcard, map, or ticket stub from your adventure. It can be anything you want—the choice is yours! Use the space below to write details or a short story about your adventure.

MY ADVENTURES JOURNAL

Today's date _____

Where I was today _____
_____

Who was with me _____
_____
_____

What the weather was like _____

What I ate _____
_____

My favorite things I saw today _____
_____
_____

My favorite things I did today _____
_____
_____

Interesting noises or smells _____
_____
_____

In the box below, draw a picture or place something like a photo, postcard, map, or ticket stub from your adventure. It can be anything you want—the choice is yours! Use the space below to write details or a short story about your adventure.

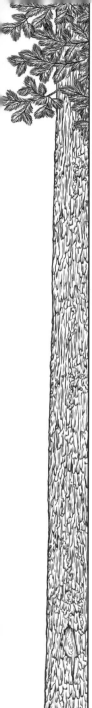

MY ADVENTURES JOURNAL

Today's date _____

Where I was today _____

_____

Who was with me _____

_____

_____

What the weather was like _____

What I ate _____

_____

My favorite things I saw today _____

_____

_____

My favorite things I did today _____

_____

_____

Interesting noises or smells _____

_____

_____

In the box below, draw a picture or place something like a photo, postcard, map, or ticket stub from your adventure. It can be anything you want—the choice is yours! Use the space below to write details or a short story about your adventure.

MY ADVENTURES STASH

Attach an envelope to this page to hold treasures you gather from your adventures —attraction ticket stubs, travel postcards and photos, drawings, a found leaf or feather from your local park*—whatever you like! When you have time, you can add your treasures to your Adventures Journal pages. Decorate your envelope with drawings, stickers, or stamps.

*IMPORTANT
Never take natural objects from national or state parks. Leave found rocks, leaves, etc. for others to enjoy.

MEET THE ANIMALS, SCAT & TRACKS

Let's get to know more about animals from the *Who Pooped?* series with fun facts and the clues they leave behind, like scat and tracks.

Scat is POOP! It's the name hikers and trackers use for animal poop, and if you can identify it, you can tell what animal has been there and when. Usually, the harder the scat is, the longer it has been there. That tells you if the animal might be close by or if it's been awhile since it has been walking where you are. Often you can also tell what the animal was eating by what you see in the poop (look but don't touch). Sounds gross, but it's pretty cool! Look for other clues while exploring, like nests and animals trails.

Tracks are animal footprints. Learning to "track" their footprints lets you know which animals have been walking where you are. Tracks are easiest to see in the snow or mud because they are soft enough for the animals' feet to sink into and leave footprints.

Now, let's meet the animals! ☑ Check the animals you've seen. Color the animals, their scat and tracks, and whatever else you want to draw and color on the pages, like where they might live, trees, flowers, puffy clouds in the sky—anything you want!

BEYOND SCAT & TRACKS—WORDS TO KNOW

CAMOUFLAGE: An animal's coloring that helps it hide from predators by blending in with its environment.

CARNIVORE: An animal that eats meat.

CARRION: The flesh of a dead animal.

CLIMATE: The weather patterns in an area, in general or over a long time.

COLONIES: Groups of an animal living in the same area.

DENNING: An animal living in a den or shelter.

DIURNAL: An animal that's active during the day and sleeps at night.

DOMESTIC: An animal that has been tamed by people so it's no longer wild.

ECOSYSTEM: All living things in an area that play a role in overall survival by interacting with each other and with non-living things like weather, water, and soil.

ELUSIVE: Animals that hide, either by night or in brush and trees, and are rarely seen by people.

ENDANGERED: Living things that are in danger of becoming extinct.

EXTINCT: Animals or plants that no longer exist.

HABITAT: An animal's natural environment or home.

HERBIVORE: An animal that eats only plants.

HIBERNATE: A deep sleep through a season, such as winter.

MAMMAL: Animals with fur or hair that are born live (not in an egg) and are fed milk from their mom when they are babies.

NOCTURNAL: An animal that's active mostly at night and sleeps during the day.

OMNIVORE: An animal that eats both plants and meat.

PREDATOR: An animal that hunts other animals for food.

PREY: An animal that is hunted for food.

QUILLS: Fused hair that forms very hard spikes, like on porcupines.

SOLITARY: Animals that prefer to live alone.

SPAWN: A fish laying eggs.

UNGULATES: Animals with hooves.

VENOMOUS: An animal that produces poison to kill its prey or to use in self-defense.

SEARCH FOR THE ANIMALS

From the *Who Pooped?* series.

G	T	C	O	Y	O	T	E	A	D	T	G	O	W	L	I	R
R	A	B	B	I	T	U	Z	U	F	B	H	T	G	A	B	I
I	S	D	A	C	D	R	A	C	C	O	O	N	J	C	A	V
Z	C	U	P	E	C	K	E	H	F	B	R	K	C	O	D	E
Z	E	A	P	D	E	E	R	I	L	C	S	L	H	I	G	R
L	V	F	G	U	Q	Y	B	P	D	A	E	A	G	L	E	O
Y	B	I	B	C	Y	X	I	M	I	T	C	M	R	H	R	T
B	H	E	L	K	W	R	H	U	F	I	S	H	E	R	C	T
E	C	R	F	B	E	A	W	N	V	J	B	I	B	C	W	E
A	O	M	D	P	H	N	S	K	U	N	K	E	E	C	E	R
R	E	I	K	I	L	P	Q	S	F	V	W	T	N	V	P	P
K	S	N	A	K	E	W	U	P	T	Y	V	K	M	Z	B	E
E	G	E	C	A	G	P	I	G	I	G	O	J	H	B	G	C
G	H	E	I	O	Z	G	R	I	N	G	T	A	I	L	Z	C
O	A	U	B	J	N	F	R	H	F	J	X	N	R	A	T	A
T	O	R	T	O	I	S	E	Q	M	R	E	X	I	C	X	R
P	Z	W	J	A	V	E	L	I	N	A	R	K	Z	K	O	Y
M	O	U	N	T	A	I	N	G	O	A	T	B	X	B	A	X
O	Q	N	P	O	R	M	O	L	S	U	L	I	Y	E	X	W
U	F	U	P	R	A	I	R	I	E	D	O	G	M	A	T	I
N	R	S	R	U	J	T	K	B	E	S	L	H	H	R	Z	L
T	V	P	O	R	C	U	P	I	N	E	C	O	A	T	I	D
A	T	Q	N	V	H	N	I	S	P	C	O	R	S	A	V	H
I	P	S	G	D	O	M	O	O	S	E	B	N	W	R	O	O
N	Q	M	H	A	R	E	J	N	W	E	A	S	E	L	F	G
L	H	F	O	H	T	K	M	L	Z	R	Q	H	V	S	P	T
I	A	W	R	V	K	B	C	T	Y	H	B	E	A	V	E	R
O	W	D	N	J	I	U	F	L	I	C	K	E	R	P	L	U
N	K	N	L	N	U	R	J	I	R	H	Y	P	K	N	I	L
Z	Y	E	X	M	A	R	M	O	T	G	V	W	L	R	C	U
K	U	M	G	B	W	O	L	F	D	X	S	C	J	E	A	F
F	O	X	L	O	A	L	C	Z	B	A	T	D	M	W	N	T

Circle the animals you find in the word search

BADGER
BAT
BEAVER
BIGHORN SHEEP
BISON
BLACK BEAR
BOBCAT
BURRO
CHIPMUNK
COATI
COYOTE
DEER
DUCK
EAGLE
ELK
ERMINE
FISHER
FLICKER
FOX
GREBE
GRIZZLY BEAR
HARE
HAWK
HORSE
JAVELINA
MARMOT
MOOSE
MOUNTAIN GOAT
MOUNTAIN LION
OWL
PECCARY
PELICAN
PIKA
PORCUPINE
PRAIRIE DOG
PRONGHORN
RABBIT
RACCOON
RAT
RINGTAIL
RIVER OTTER
SKUNK
SNAKE
SQUIRREL
TORTOISE
TURKEY
WEASEL
WILD HOG
WOLF

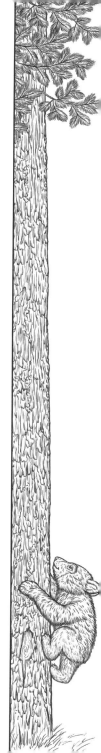

WHERE THE ANIMALS ARE*

*From sites featured in the *Who Pooped?* series. Many of these animals, like ducks and chipmunks, are not only found at the locations listed below. They can also be seen in national, state, and local parks and other habitats across the country.

☑ Check the *Who Pooped?* sites you've visited and the animals you've seen, and use the line underneath to write where you saw a *Who Pooped?* animal.

☐ Olympic National Park
☐ Glacier National Park
☐ Acadia National Park
☐ Cascades
☐ Yellowstone National Park
☐ Black Hills
☐ Northwoods
☐ Central Park
☐ Grand Teton National Park
☐ Redwoods
☐ Red Rock Canyon National Conservation Area
☐ Rocky Mountain National Park
☐ Yosemite National Park
☐ Colorado Plateau
☐ Shenandoah National Park
☐ Sequoia/Kings Canyon National Park
☐ Grand Canyon National Park
☐ Death Valley National Park
☐ Great Smoky Mountains National Park
☐ Sonoran Desert
☐ Big Bend National Park

☐ **BADGER:** Death Valley, Glacier, Grand Teton, Yellowstone

☐ **BAT:** Acadia, Cascades, Grand Canyon, Olympic, Sequoia / Kings Canyon, Shenandoah, Yosemite

☐ **BEAVER:** Glacier, Grand Teton, Great Smoky Mountains, Northwoods, Redwoods

☐ **BIGHORN SHEEP:** Death Valley, Red Rock Canyon, Rocky Mountain

☐ **BISON:** Black Hills, Grand Teton, Yellowstone

☐ **BLACK BEAR:** Acadia, Big Bend, Great Smoky Mountains, Northwoods, Olympic, Redwoods, Rocky Mountain, Sequoia / Kings Canyon, Shenandoah, Yosemite

☐ **BOBCAT:** Death Valley, Grand Canyon, Northwoods, Sequoia / Kings Canyon, Shenandoah, Yosemite

☐ **BURRO:** Black Hills, Red Rock Canyon, Sonoran Desert

☐ **CHIPMUNK:** Acadia, Central Park

☐ **COYOTE:** Acadia, Big Bend, Black Hills, Cascades, Colorado Plateau, Death Valley, Glacier, Grand Canyon, Grand Teton, Great Smoky Mountains, Olympic, Red Rock Canyon, Rocky Mountain, Sequoia / Kings Canyon, Sonoran Desert, Yosemite

☐ **DEER:** Acadia, Big Bend, Black Hills, Cascades, Colorado Plateau, Glacier, Grand Canyon, Grand Teton, Great Smoky Mountains, Northwoods, Olympic, Rocky Mountain, Sequoia / Kings Canyon, Shenandoah, Sonoran Desert, Yellowstone, Yosemite

☐ **DOG:** Central Park

☐ **DUCK:** Death Valley

☐ **EAGLE:** Cascades, Colorado Plateau

☐ **ELK:** Glacier, Grand Teton, Olympic, Redwoods, Rocky Mountain, Yellowstone

- ☐ FISHER: Redwoods

- ☐ FLICKER: Red Rock Canyon

- ☐ FOX: Acadia, Big Bend, Colorado Plateau, Redwoods

- ☐ GOOSE: Central Park

- ☐ GREBE: Death Valley

- ☐ GRIZZLY BEAR: Glacier, Grand Teton, Yellowstone

- ☐ GROUNDHOG: Central Park

- ☐ HAWK: Central Park, Redwoods

- ☐ HORSE: Big Bend, Central Park, Glacier, Grand Teton, Rocky Mountain, Sequoia / Kings Canyon, Shenandoah, Yellowstone, Yosemite

- ☐ JAVELINA / PECCARY (WILD HOG): Big Bend, Grand Canyon, Great Smoky Mountains, Sonoran Desert

- ☐ MARMOT: Rocky Mountain

- ☐ MOOSE: Grand Teton, Northwoods, Yellowstone

- ☐ MOUNTAIN GOAT: Glacier

- ☐ MOUNTAIN LION: Big Bend, Black Hills, Cascades, Colorado Plateau, Death Valley, Glacier, Grand Canyon, Olympic, Red Rock Canyon, Redwoods, Rocky Mountain, Sequoia / Kings Canyon, Sonoran Desert, Yellowstone, Yosemite

- ☐ MUSKRAT: Central Park

- ☐ OWL: Acadia, Big Bend, Cascades, Grand Canyon, Northwoods, Olympic, Red Rock Canyon, Rocky Mountain, Sequoia / Kings Canyon, Shenandoah, Sonoran Desert, Yosemite

- ☐ PELICAN: Redwoods

- ☐ PIKA: Cascades

- ☐ PORCUPINE: Black Hills, Colorado Plateau, Grand Canyon, Sequoia / Kings Canyon

- ☐ PRAIRIE DOG: Black Hills

- ☐ PRONGHORN: Black Hills

- ☐ RABBIT / HARE: Acadia, Big Bend, Black Hills, Cascades, Colorado Plateau, Death Valley, Glacier, Grand Canyon, Grand Teton, Great Smoky Mountains, Northwoods, Red Rock Canyon, Rocky Mountain, Sequoia / Kings Canyon, Shenandoah, Sonoran Desert, Yellowstone

- ☐ RACCOON: Acadia, Central Park, Olympic, Shenandoah

- ☐ RAT: Central Park, Red Rock Canyon

- ☐ RINGTAIL / COATI: Big Bend, Grand Canyon, Sonoran Desert

- ☐ RIVER OTTER: Acadia

- ☐ SKUNK: Great Smoky Mountains, Redwoods

- ☐ SNAKE: Colorado Plateau, Death Valley, Red Rock Canyon

- ☐ SQUIRREL: Cascades, Central Park, Colorado Plateau, Olympic, Redwoods, Shenandoah, Yosemite

- ☐ TORTOISE: Red Rock Canyon, Sonoran Desert

- ☐ TURKEY: Black Hills, Great Smoky Mountains, Northwoods, Shenandoah

- ☐ WEASEL / ERMINE: Cascades, Northwoods, Olympic

- ☐ WOLF: Northwoods, Yellowstone

❑ CHIPMUNK

Chipmunks are the smallest member of the squirrel family—most are only seven to eight inches long! Their coats can vary from gray to reddish-brown to brown. You can find chipmunks all over the United States, from forests to deserts to backyards with bird feeders. Chipmunks hibernate in cold areas and must gather food to survive through the winter. They eat insects, nuts, seeds, berries, mushrooms, and grains and prefer to gather food where they have some cover to hide from predators.

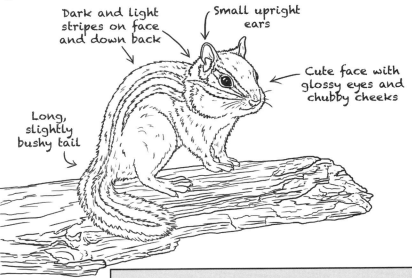

Dark and light stripes on face and down back

Small upright ears

Cute face with glossy eyes and chubby cheeks

Long, slightly bushy tail

Chipmunk scat is hard and shaped like tiny, long ovals

Chipmunk tracks show four toes on the front and five on the back

FUN FACTS

- Chipmunks have pouches inside their cheeks to gather and carry food home.
- They can be very talkative and make a wide variety of calls, including chirping that sounds like birds!
- Their homes vary depending on where they live. Some make nests in bushes or logs and some burrow underground with separate "rooms" for storing food, sleeping, and having babies.
- One chipmunk can gather up to 160 nuts in a day!
- Chipmunk babies are called pups and are about the size of a jelly bean!

❑ GOLDEN-MANTLED GROUND SQUIRREL

Golden-mantled ground squirrels look like giant chipmunks! They are usually eight to twelve inches long. They get their name from the golden color on their head and shoulders. Like chipmunks, they have dark and light stripes that go down their back, but they don't have stripes on their faces. Instead, they have white rings around their eyes. These ground squirrels live in the western part of the United States and eat nuts, seeds, berries, mushrooms, pinecones, leaves, flowers, grains, bird eggs, insects, and sometimes carrion.

No stripes on face, white rings around eyes

Golden color on head and shoulders

Dark and light stripes on back similar to chipmunks

Golden-mantled ground squirrel scat is hard and shaped like long ovals

Golden-mantled ground squirrel tracks show four toes on the front and five on the back

FUN FACTS

- Like chipmunks, golden-mantled ground squirrels carry food in their cheeks until they can get home to their burrows. They also dig holes to hide food in the ground to save for a later meal.
- They are usually quiet unless scared and then will make a loud chirping sound. If they are ready to fight, they will growl!
- Golden-mantled squirrels clean themselves by rolling in the dirt! Afterwards, they use their front paws and teeth to "brush" their fur.
- A male is called a buck and a female is called a doe. Babies are called pups, kits, or kittens.

❏ PIKA

Even though pikas look like tiny hamsters, only six to eight inches long, they are actually in the rabbit family! They live in high, rocky mountain areas near alpine meadows and make their homes in rock piles. They are very busy little creatures and are usually seen gathering plants to dry and stack for later, which is called "haystacking." Since they do not hibernate, they need to stash a lot of dried plants in their dens to eat during the long, cold winters.

Large, round ears

Small, round body with brown fur

Most often seen gathering food

Tail too small to see

Pika scat is very small, hard, brown balls

Pika tracks have five toes on the front and four on the back

FUN FACTS

- Pikas make a wide variety of calls to communicate with other pikas.
- Even though they live in colonies with other pikas, they are very territorial and protect their den and the food they gathered for winter.
- Pikas have very good hearing, which helps them hear when predators are near.
- Pikas cannot live in hot temperatures. As climates get warmer, pikas move to higher, cooler elevations if they can.
- Pikas are sometimes called "rock rabbits!"

❑ RABBIT & HARE

Rabbits and hares are in the same family, but they are actually different species. They look very similar with long ears, fluffy short tails, long feet, and eyes on the sides of their head that can rotate so they can see all around to watch for predators. But hares are bigger, their ears are taller, their hind feet are larger—and they are much faster! Another difference is that rabbits (except cottontails) make their homes and have babies in underground burrows with rooms, but hares and cottontails give birth and make their homes in aboveground nests.

Hares are larger and have longer ears that are usually black-tipped

Hares' fur can change according to the season—grayish-brown fur can turn white in winter

Rabbits' fur usually stays the same color all year and can be white, tan, brown, gray, or black

Smaller body and ears, rounder face

Longer legs

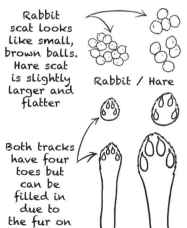

Rabbit scat looks like small, brown balls. Hare scat is slightly larger and flatter

Rabbit / Hare

Both tracks have four toes but can be filled in due to the fur on their feet

FUN FACTS

- Hares can run fast—up to 45 miles per hour!
- Rabbits' front teeth never stop growing!
- Both rabbits and hares are herbivores.
- Rabbits are very common and are found in most states. They are also popular pets.
- Hare babies are born with fur and open eyes, but rabbit babies are born naked with closed eyes.
- Rabbit babies are called kittens or kits, but hare babies are called leverets. That's a funny name!
- Rabbits can have up to 25 kits a year!

❑ SKUNK

Skunks live all over the United States, from forests to deserts, even in cities and neighborhoods. Skunks are unique in that they leave another clue besides scat and tracks—the smell of their spray, called musk, which can be very stinky and last for days! So even if you don't see a skunk, you may smell where it has been. Skunks spray when they think they are in danger. Sometimes they give you a warning first by turning around, stomping their feet, and growling. But when they lift their tail, watch out!

Long, fluffy tail

Most skunks have black fur with one or two white stripes

*Animals that have been sprayed will remember the distinctive markings and stay away

Spray comes from the base of its tail

Small ears

Skunk scat has a tube shape and may have pieces of insects, hair, or berries in it

Skunk tracks have five toes with claw marks

FUN FACTS

- A skunk can spray its stinky, oily spray up to 12 feet, so you want to stay far away from these cute critters!
- Skunks are nocturnal, usually looking for food at night and sleeping during the day.
- Skunks are omnivores. In addition to eating plants and meat, they also like to eat honeybees!
- A male skunk is called a buck and a female is called a doe—just like deer and elk. Babies are called kits.

❏ PORCUPINE

Porcupines are not related to the skunk—they are in the same family as mice and beavers—but just like the skunk, you want to stay away from them! They have sharp quills for protection. Like the skunk, they will often give a warning by stomping their feet and hissing. Then their quills fan out from their body and the porcupines will charge, swatting their short spiky tail at their predator! Porcupines are found in our western and northern states, mostly living in forests, but can also be found in grasslands and deserts.

Black to goldish-brown hair with lighter-colored quills

Sharp quills for protection from predators

Small head and ears

Porcupine scat is oval like jelly beans, about an inch long

Porcupine tracks show four toes on the front and five on the back

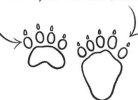

FUN FACTS

- Porcupines have up to 30,000 quills!
- They don't really throw their quills. The quills detach and lodge into the skin of their predators. The quill's barbs make them hard to remove, painful, and sometimes deadly!
- Porcupines are nocturnal.
- They are herbivores and enjoy eating tree bark, sticks, leaves, and grasses.
- Baby porcupines are called porcupettes.

❏ BEAVER

Beavers are very busy! With their strong teeth and jaws, they chew lots of branches and can chew down a whole tree! They use wood mixed with mud to build dome-shaped homes, called lodges, and dams in streams. The dams block the water from flowing downstream, which creates wetlands, a nice pond for swimming, and a moat around their lodge for protection. More at home in the water than on land, they have large webbed back feet, which make them excellent swimmers, and their thick fur is oily and waterproof, which allows them to swim comfortably in icy cold water.

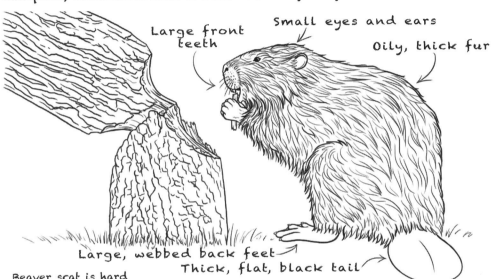

Large front teeth

Small eyes and ears

Oily, thick fur

Large, webbed back feet

Thick, flat, black tail

Beaver scat is hard to find since it is usually in the water. It is round or oval and has pieces of wood in it

Beaver tracks are also rarely seen because their tail and any wood they are dragging often wipes them away

Back feet are webbed

FUN FACTS

- Beavers' front teeth never stop growing!
- They are herbivores that like to eat leaves, bark, and water plants.
- They can swim underwater for up to 15 minutes without coming up for air and have third eyelids that are clear, like goggles, that allow them to see underwater.
- Beavers slap the water with their big flat tail to signal danger.
- Beavers are mostly nocturnal, building and maintaining their dens at night.

❏ RIVER OTTER

River otters, like beavers, love to swim! As amphibious mammals, their streamlined bodies with long, straight tails are built to move quicky and easily through the water. They are very playful creatures, often seen chasing each other, playing, wrestling, and sliding down riverbanks. Otters have two layers of fur—the outer layer is waterproof and the inner layer is soft and cozy—as well as a layer of fat that keeps them from freezing in cold and icy water.

Playful and affectionate

Brown-gray fur

Small head, eyes, and ears

Lighter neck and underside

Love to swim!

Short legs with webbed feet

Long, strong tail

Otter scat has bones and scales in it from the fish they eat

Otter tracks have five toes. You may or may not be able to see its claws and webbed toes

FUN FACTS

- Otters are made for water and can hold their breath for up to eight minutes! They can also close their ears and nose when swimming, and they have also have third, clear eyelids that allow them to see underwater.
- Their long, strong tails and webbed back feet help them swim and dive very fast and deep—down to 60 feet!
- Otters haves long whiskers that sense movement in the water. This helps them find fish, frogs, small mammals, and shellfish to eat.
- You can find river otters across the country in lakes, rivers, streams, wetlands, and even the ocean.

❑ RACCOON

Called "masked bandits," raccoons are very smart and clever—and can get into a lot of trouble! Always on the search for food, they are known to turn over trash cans, get into pet food, open latches on gates, and eat from your garden. They are easy to recognize because of their famous black mask on their face with white eyebrows and fur around the nose. The rest of their body is gray and brown, and they have a ring-striped tail. Raccoons live throughout the country, preferring forests where they can make their homes in hollow trees, but you may also find them in your neighborhood.

Famous black mask with white eyebrows and white around nose

Brown to gray fur

Striped tail

Front paws are similar to people hands

Raccoon scat is tubular and may contain roundworm eggs which can infect people and pets. Stay away!

Raccoon tracks look hand-like with small claws

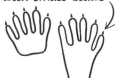

FUN FACTS

- Raccoons are omnivores and will eat just about anything—fruit, nuts, eggs, birds, frogs, and fish.
- They are nocturnal, scavenging for food mostly at night.
- Raccoon hands look and work a lot like people hands. They can open things like doors, jars, and trash cans, and are very good climbers.
- Their black mask doesn't just look cool, it actually helps them see better by absorbing light and reducing glare.
- A raccoon named Rebecca used to live at the White House!

❏ RINGTAIL & COATI

Ringtails and coatis are members of the raccoon family and are primarily found in the Southwest. The ringtail is very elusive, so you may never see one. Its body is much smaller than a raccoon or coati, about the size of a squirrel. It has a small head with large eyes, white mask, large pink ears, and a very big, fluffy, black-and-white- ringed tail that it uses for balance when climbing. The coati has a long body, a mask on its face, a long thin tail, and a long nose it uses to find food in the dirt, leaves, and under rocks.

RINGTAIL

Small head with large black eyes, a white mask, and large ears

Short legs

Big, black-and-white, fluffy tail can be longer than its body

COATI

Long, thin, ringed tail is upright when walking

Brown fur

Small ears with white around eyes and long nose

Sharp claws

Scat for both is usually tube-shaped

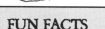

Ringtail / Coati

Tracks for both have five toes. Coati claws are longer.

FUN FACTS

- Ringtails are nocturnal like raccoons, but coatis are diurnal.
- Ringtails prefer homes in caves or hollow trees in rocky canyons, and coatis sleep in trees—sometimes in a nest!
- Female coatis are social and live with many other coatis in a pack or band, but ringtails are solitary.
- Coatis and ringtails are omnivores and like to eat fruit, nuts, insects, eggs, and small mammals and reptiles.

❏ BOBCAT

Bobcats were once endangered, but in the 1970s, laws were created to protect them. Now there are many bobcats, but you will probably never see one even though they live in a variety of habitats, from forests to marshes to deserts, and even in the outskirts of some cities. Bobcats are very good hunters and eat birds and small animals, like rabbits—but they can also take down a large deer! They often cover their food to save for later meals. Bobcats prefer to make their main home in a rocky den that offers protection, like a cave, but they can also have other dens in their territory for shelter while hunting, like a hollow tree trunk.

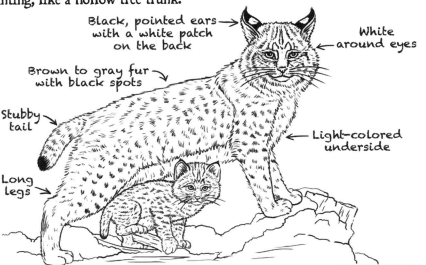

Black, pointed ears → with a white patch on the back

White ← around eyes

Brown to gray fur → with black spots

Stubby tail →

← Light-colored underside

Long legs →

Bobcat scat is often broken into pieces and buried

About half the size of mountain lion paws, bobcat tracks have four toes and usually no claw marks

FUN FACTS

- A mama bobcat can have one to six spotted kittens.
- They are about twice the size of the average domestic cats that live in our homes.
- Bobcats get their name from their stubby tail, which at only 6 to 7 inches is shorter than most cats'.
- Like most cats, they are very good climbers and will often climb trees to get away from danger or to pounce on their prey from above.
- Bobcats are very athletic. They can jump as high as 12 feet and run up to 34 miles per hour!

❑ MOUNTAIN LION

Mountain lions are called many names: cougar, panther, puma, and catamount, among others—and in fact, they hold the Guinness World Record for the most names! They can live in just about any habitat and used to live all over the United States but now are found mostly in the western states. Like bobcats, they are elusive. They are the largest wildcats in the country, up to nine feet long and almost 200 pounds. They are top predators, and like the bobcat, they will bury their food under leaves and dirt to eat later.

Black on the back of the ears and on each side of its muzzle

Golden, to reddish brown, to gray fur

Black on the tip of its tail

Cream-colored throat, chest, and belly

Large paws

Mountain lion scat is usually buried and has bone and fur in it

Mountain lion tracks have four toes and usually no claw marks

FUN FACTS

- Even though they are called mountain **LIONS**, they don't roar—but they do purr like your kitty at home.
- They usually have two to four babies called kittens or cubs. They are born with spots and blue eyes but grow out of them when they are about nine months old.
- Mountain lions are sometimes called "Ghost Cats" since they are rarely seen.
- They have powerful hind legs that enable them to jump up to 45 feet forward, 15 feet high, and run up to 50 miles per hour. That's as fast as a car!

❏ RED FOX & KIT FOX

Foxes are the smallest members of the wild canine (dog) family. The red fox is the largest of the foxes and the most well known since it is common throughout the United States. It is very smart and has learned to live and hunt in many different environments, including prairies, forests, deserts, and sometimes farms and our neighborhoods. Kit foxes, often called desert foxes, are the smallest of the fox family and usually live in the Southwest, although some live as far north as Oregon.

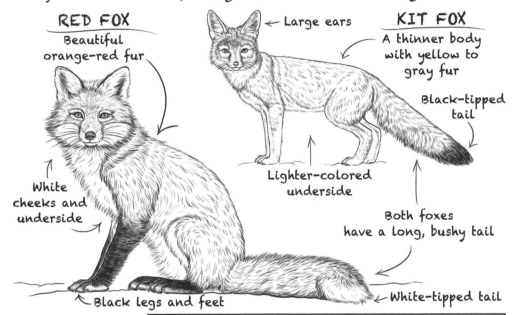

RED FOX
Beautiful orange-red fur

Large ears

KIT FOX
A thinner body with yellow to gray fur

Black-tipped tail

White cheeks and underside

Lighter-colored underside

Both foxes have a long, bushy tail

Black legs and feet

White-tipped tail

Fox scat is tube-shaped and tapered on the ends. Since they are omnivores, it may have pieces of bones, hair, insects, or fruit and seeds

FUN FACTS

- Foxes have very good eyesight. Their eyes have vertical slits like cats, which help them see in the dark.
- Male foxes are called dogs and females are called vixens. Their babies are called pups.
- Foxes have large ears and excellent hearing, and can hear animals moving under the ground and deep snow.
- Foxes are nocturnal so usually hunt at night and sleep during the day.
- Foxes can run very fast—up to 45 miles per hour!

❏ GRAY FOX & ARCTIC FOX

The gray fox is one of the larger foxes, although not as large as the red fox. It is also found throughout the United States though is hard to see because it hides in bushes or thick woodlands. The artic fox has very thick fur that keeps it warm in the extreme cold weather of the Arctic. Its fur camouflages with its environment, turning white in the winter to blend in with the snow, then changing to brown or gray to blend with the brush in spring and summer.

ARCTIC FOX
Thick all-white fur in the winter

GRAY FOX
Fur is salt-and-pepper gray on top

Shorter nose and legs

Long, bushy tail

White cheeks and throat

Long claws

Reddish-brown stomach, chest, and legs

Tail is very long and not quite as bushy

Tail has black stripe on top and black-tipped end

Fox tracks have four toes with claw marks, with the exception of the gray fox that can retract its claws

*Since red and arctic foxes are very furry, it may be hard to see the details of their tracks

FUN FACTS

- The gray fox can climb trees!
- Foxes are omnivores. They prefer to eat small mammals but also eat birds, fish, insects, and fruit. Arctic foxes often follow polar bears to eat their leftovers.
- Foxes burrow underground to make a home called a den where they hide from predators and stay cool on hot days and warm on cold days.
- Experts think the gray fox is the oldest fox species in the world—maybe 10 million years old!

❑ COYOTE

Coyotes are known for being very clever—a reputation that largely started from Native American stories passed down through generations. Their ability to easily adapt to different habitats and foods to survive proves they are indeed clever. Coyotes can be found all over the United States in prairies, deserts, forests, mountains, and the outskirts of towns and cities. They prefer to eat small mammals like rabbits and rodents, but will eat birds, fish, and snakes, as well as grass, fruit, and berries. For smaller prey, coyotes usually hunt alone but will hunt in a group for larger animals like deer.

Long, bushy tail with black tip that stays down when running

Gray, brown, or tan fur

← Large, triangle-shaped ears that stand up

← Long, pointy muzzle (nose)

Playful pups!

Coyote scat is tapered on ends and shinier than wolf scat. It usually contains hair and bone from smaller animals

Coyote tracks have four toes with claw marks

FUN FACTS

- Coyote moms have large litters, from three to twelve pups. The dad helps take care of the pups.
- They are sometimes called prairie or brush wolves.
- A coyote often makes its home, called a den, out of another animal's home.
- Coyotes communicate with a wide variety of calls and have great senses of vision, hearing, and smell. Like foxes, they can hear and smell animals under dirt and snow.
- Coyotes are great swimmers and also can run up to 40 miles per hour!

❑ WOLF

Wolves and coyotes are in the same family, the canine family, like foxes. Although they have similar fur coats and body shape, wolves have smaller ears, wider noses, and larger bodies. Gray wolves, also called timber wolves, used to be found all over the United States, but they were hunted and became endangered. After understanding that wolves are very important for the ecosystem, they were protected and reintroduced to places like Yellowstone National Park. Wolves are very social animals and live in family units called packs to protect each other, raise their pups, and hunt together.

Slightly shorter, → rounded ears

Overall fur can be gray, black, brown, tan, or white

Darker gray-brown fur on back

Wider nose →

Cute, furry puppies!

Lighter fur on underside

Long, slightly bushy tail

Wolf scat has bits of hair from larger animals

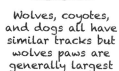

Wolves, coyotes, and dogs all have similar tracks but wolves paws are generally largest

FUN FACTS

- A wolf's howl can be heard up to six miles away!
- Wolves are carnivores, top predators that are smart and strong. They have great senses, and when working together, can hunt large animals like elk and moose.
- Wolves can run up to 40 miles per hour, and can run for a very long time, allowing them to outrun most prey.
- Wolves are the largest member of the dog family, weighing up to 200 pounds!

❏ MOUNTAIN GOAT

Found in Alaska, the northern Cascade and Rocky Mountains, and as a small intro-duced population in the Black Hills, mountain goats are expert climbers most often seen on steep, rocky cliffs and ledges at high elevations—far away from predators that can't climb as well. In addition, their white fur helps hide them by camouflaging with the white snow. Mountain goat hooves are hard on the outside but have soft centers that help them grip on rocks when climbing.

Sharp horns slightly curve back

Fluffy white fur

Short tail

Black, split hooves called cloven

Mountain goat scat varies depending on the season— in winter it is dry, hard pellets,

in summer scat is in a wet pile of soft pellets

Mountain goat tracks are two ovals from their two-toed hooves

FUN FACTS

- In the winter, mountain goats have two layers of fur to keep warm. In warm months, the outer layer falls off.
- Babies are called kids, males are called billies, and females are called nannies and usually only have one kid at a time.
- Kids start climbing as early as one day old!
- Males and females look very similar—both have horns and beards. Billies are larger and usually live alone, while nannies live with the kids in groups called bands.
- Scientists can count how old they are by the rings on their horns—like counting the rings in a tree trunk!

☐ BIGHORN SHEEP

Bighorn sheep get their name from the large, curved horns on the males. Females have smaller horns with very little curve. Bighorn sheep live in the mountains and deserts of western states, but the largest bighorns live in the Rocky Mountain region from Canada to Mexico. Like mountain goats, bighorn sheep are expert climbers and go to higher elevations to stay away from predators.

They may break the tips off their horns to see better →

← Males have large curved horns

Brown to gray fur →

Ewes have only a small curve in horns ↘

All have white around nose

White behind and back of legs

Split hooves for climbing

Bighorn sheep scat is dry oval pellets with a point on one end

Bighorn sheep tracks are ovals that have straighter edges on the sides

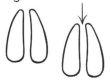

FUN FACTS

- Bighorn sheep males are called rams, the females are called ewes, and the babies are called lambs.
- During the fall, males "ram" their horns together repeatedly to decide who will be the boss ram and get the girls.
- Ewes live in large nursery herds to care for and protect the lambs. Rams live in smaller boys-only herds.
- Bighorn sheep and mountain goats are herbivores.
- Some rams grow horns so big they weigh more than all the bones in their body together—up to 30 pounds!

❏ PRONGHORN

Pronghorn are often called antelope, but they are really their own species. They get their name from the male's "pronged" horns that branch out to two points. Pronghorn have true horns that shed every year. These animals are built for running, with long, thin, strong legs. They are the fastest land mammal in North America. Pronghorn usually live in grasslands of central and western states, although they can also be found in deserts.

Black "pronged" horns

Bucks have black markings on their face

Does have short horns that are not pronged.

Large eyes →

Red-brown fur

White behind with small tail

White neck bands and underside

Long legs for running

Pronghorn scat pellets stick together

Pronghorn tracks are in two parts like deer, but come to curved points at the top

FUN FACTS

- Male pronghorn are called bucks, females are called does (rhymes with nose), and babies are called fawns.
- Both bucks and does have horns, but female horns are very small.
- They are herbivores and love to eat grasses, sagebrush, and other plants.
- Pronghorns can run up to 65 miles per hour, and can run a long time. Even fawns can outrun a human when they are only a few days old!

❏ DEER

The most common deer in the United States are white-tailed deer and mule deer. Most mule deer live west of the Rocky Mountains and white-tailed deer are more common in the east, although there are some areas that have both. Easy ways to remember the difference between the two deer are that mule deer have larger ears, like mules, and white-tails have larger tails that are white on the underside—they lift them up when they sense danger and it looks like they have white tails as they run away. Deer prefer to live at the edge of forests so they can hide from predators in the trees and look for food in open grassland areas.

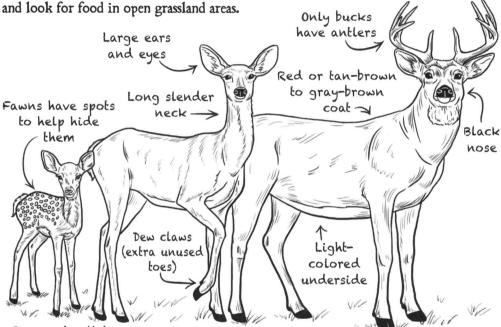

Only bucks have antlers

Large ears and eyes

Long slender neck →

Red or tan-brown to gray-brown coat

Fawns have spots to help hide them

Black nose

Dew claws (extra unused toes)

Light-colored underside

Deer scat pellets vary—they can be separate or stuck together

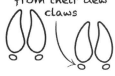

Deer tracks show split hooves, and if the ground was soft, you will see marks from their dew claws

FUN FACTS

- Deer have very good eyesight and senses of hearing and smell, making it hard to sneak up on them.
- Males are called bucks, females are called does, and babies are called fawns. Large bucks are sometimes called stags.
- Deer are herbivores that like to eat fruit, nuts, leaves, grasses—and sometimes flowers from your garden!
- A buck's antlers fall off in winter and regrow in spring.

☐ ELK

Elk are in the same family with deer and moose. They are larger than deer but not as large as moose. Like them, the males have large antlers that fall off in winter or early spring, and then regrow. A bull elk's antlers can branch out up to four feet wide! Males use their antlers to fight other males, and they make a loud call called a bugle to attract the girls. Most live in mountain forests and forest-edge meadows and valleys in western states. Native Americans called elk "wapiti," which means light-colored rump. Some people also call them red deer.

Bulls grow very large antlers!

Cows do not have antlers

Coat is tan in summer and brown in winter with a light beige rump

Calves have spots for camouflage

Shaggy mane on neck

Head, neck, stomach, and legs are darker brown

Elk scat pellets are larger than deer scat and in piles

Elk tracks show split hooves and are larger than deer tracks

FUN FACTS

- Male elk are called bulls, females are called cows, and babies are called calves.
- Elk live in large groups called herds or gangs.
- Elk are herbivores that like to eat grasses, flowers, and tree bark.
- Elk, like deer and moose, have four parts to their stomach and must re-chew their food to digest it, which is called "chewing the cud."

❏ MOOSE

Moose are the largest member of the deer family and the second-largest land animal in the United States. A moose can weigh up to 1,500 pounds! Like elk, a male's antlers can grow huge—up to six feet wide! Their antlers also fall off in the winter and then grow back larger the next spring. This is to conserve energy during the winter months. Moose prefer cool weather so live in forested areas in Alaska, some northern states, and as far south as Utah.

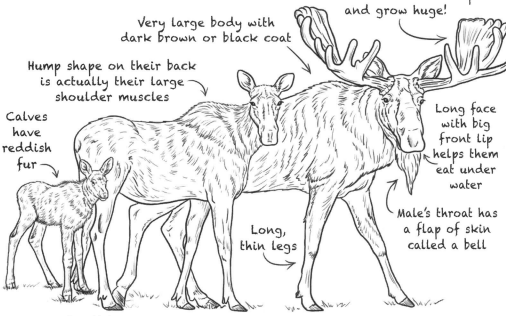

Antlers on males are "hand-shaped" and grow huge!

Very large body with dark brown or black coat

Hump shape on their back is actually their large shoulder muscles

Calves have reddish fur

Long face with big front lip helps them eat under water

Male's throat has a flap of skin called a bell

Long, thin legs

Moose scat pellets are larger than deer scat

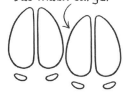

Moose tracks are similar to others in the deer family, but much larger

FUN FACTS

- Moose are found near water because they like to eat marsh and pond plants. They can swim for many miles.
- Moose are herbivores that like to eat plants like grasses, shrubs, bark, pinecones, and water plants.
- Like elk, male moose are called bulls, females are called cows, and babies are called calves.
- Moose run up to 35 miles per hour! A calf can run faster than a person when it is only five days old!

❏ BURRO

"Burro" is the Spanish name for donkey and is usually used for the wild donkeys that run free in dry, hot places like deserts in the southwestern United States. They are in the horse family but are shorter and stockier than horses, very sure-footed and hardy, able to survive in harsh conditions without much water. These qualities have made them excellent pack animals for explorers, prospectors, and pioneers traveling west since the early 1800s.

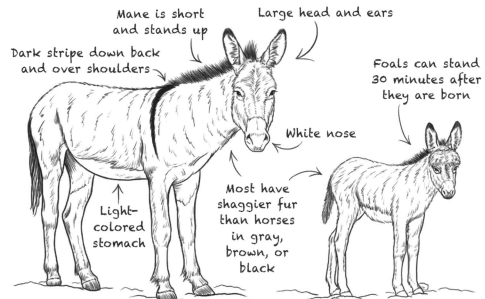

Mane is short and stands up

Large head and ears

Dark stripe down back and over shoulders

Foals can stand 30 minutes after they are born

White nose

Light-colored stomach

Most have shaggier fur than horses in gray, brown, or black

Burro scat is in large, chunky piles—you can often see bits of plants in it

A burro track shows that the round hoof is not split in two

FUN FACTS

- Male burros are called jacks, females are called jennies or jennets, and babies are called foals.

- When they sense danger, burros will often stand still and decide what's best to do rather than automatically run like horses and members of the deer family.

- Burros like to eat grasses, shrubs, and desert plants. They have tougher stomachs than horses.

- Burros can survive losing up to 30% of their body's water weight, whereas people get very dehydrated losing 10%.

❏ HORSE

Wild horses, sometimes called mustangs, mostly live in grasslands of western states, but some live on East Coast beaches and islands. People domesticated horses for transportation and work over 5,000 years ago! Horses are extremely intelligent and have very good memories. Domestic horses are sensitive and affectionate, growing to love their people as much as their people love them!

✳Horses can have many different color coats

Long, flowing tail and mane

A foal can stand up as soon as an hour after birth

Long, narrow face

Long legs

Like burros, horse scat is in large, chunky piles with bits of plants in it

Horse tracks are round, or U-shaped, like burros

FUN FACTS

- Horses can run fast—up to 55 miles per hour!
- Horses breathe only through their noses, not their mouths.
- Male horses are called stallions, females are called mares, and babies are called foals. A male foal is called a colt and a female is a filly. Small full-grown horses are called ponies.
- Horses like to eat hay, grasses, and leaves.
- Horses can sleep standing up!
- When a male burro and a female horse have a baby, it is a mule, but when a male horse and female burro have a baby, it is called a hinny.

❏ BLACK BEAR

Black bears are the smallest and most common bears in North America. Even though they are considered medium-sized bears, they can weigh over 500 pounds! They are found not only in forests, meadows, and open tundra, but also in farmlands and swamps. They have shorter claws than grizzly bears, which make them better at climbing trees. Black bears are omnivores that eat mostly fruit, nuts, and other plants, but also like to eat eggs, fish, small mammals, insects, and honey!

Black bear cubs climb trees to be safe from predators

No large shoulder hump

Straight face

Tall, rounded ears

Small, rounded claws

Scat can be piles or large tubes, depending on what the bear has eaten

Tracks are large with five visible toes and claws

FUN FACTS

- Black bears can run really fast—30 miles per hour!
- Black bears love to swim and catch fish. Even young bear cubs can swim!
- They hibernate in the winter in their dens, which sometimes can be high up in a hollow tree.
- A black bear's coat isn't always black, it can be shades of gray, brown, or tan.
- Male bears are called boars, females are called sows, and babies are called cubs.

☐ GRIZZLY BEAR

Grizzly bears, also called North American brown bears, can weigh up to 1,400 pounds! They have large claws that can be as long as an adult human's fingers. Their claw marks can be seen high on trees, which is a clue that they can climb trees if they need to, although they can't climb as well as black bears. The best way to tell if a bear is a grizzly is by the hump on its shoulders, which black bears don't have. Grizzlies can be found in forests and valleys, often near rivers where they go fishing.

Cubs are playful and like to climb on their mom

Hump on shoulders

Black, brown, or blond shaggy fur

Dished face

Bears can stand up on two legs like people

Long, sharp claws

Grizzly bear scat varies depending on what it has been eating

Grizzlies have very big tracks with long claws that can be easily seen

FUN FACTS

- The hump on a grizzly's shoulders is actually a large muscle that helps it dig for food and a den to sleep in. Grizzly bears dig more than any other bear.
- Momma bears will kill to protect their babies!
- Like black bears, grizzlies hibernate through winter and must eat a lot of food to gain fat before denning.
- Grizzly bears are omnivores that eat plants, meat, and insects—and they love moths!
- A grizzly can be eight feet tall when it stands up on its two back legs like a human!

❏ BISON

The American bison is the largest land animal in the United States, and America's national mammal! Often called a buffalo, it is actually not related to true buffalos and is in the same family as goats, cattle, and sheep. They used to roam our country from the Great Plains to the forests and were very important to Plains Indians. But in the 1800s, bison were overhunted, almost becoming extinct. Today, Yellowstone National Park is the only place in the country to have been home to bison since prehistoric times!

Tail with tuft of fur at end

Shaggy brown fur

Males and females have horns

Hump on shoulders

Big head with mane and beard

Calves are reddish-orange

Bison scat is in large piles with grasses in it

Bison tracks are large and more rounded than other hoofed animals like moose and deer

FUN FACTS

- The hump on its shoulders give the bison the strength to push through snow with its head to find food.
- A bison often raises its tail as a sign that it is going to charge. Don't get close or plan on outrunning a bison—it can run up to 40 miles per hour!
- Males are called bulls, females are called cows, and babies are called calves. Bison calves are sometimes called "red dogs" because they are reddish-orange when young.
- A male bison can weigh up to 2,000 pounds!

MY ANIMAL FIELD JOURNAL

Wherever you are, whether it is in a national or state park, in the desert or mountains, in a local park or a zoo, or in the city, your neighborhood, or your own backyard, you are bound to see animals or their clues.

In this section, journal about your own animal sightings and clue findings. Here are some ideas for your animal journal:

- Draw a picture or attach a photo of an animal you saw.
- Write notes of your observations—it's a great way to study animals!
- How big was it? What color was it? What was it doing? Did it make any sounds? Was it alone or with other animals? What was its habitat like?
- Record "clues" you found that an animal left behind, like scat or tracks. You can draw or take a picture of that too!
- How big was the scat or track? (There's a ruler on the back cover to help you measure it.) What color was the scat? Was it hard or soft? (You can poke it with a stick to find out.) What animal do you think left it? Was there anything interesting about it? Scat and tracks can tell you so much without even seeing the animal!

*REMEMBER: Always keep your distance from wild animals. Wildlife is wild and can hurt you! Binoculars are great for observing animals without getting too close.

ANIMAL SIGHTING OR CLUE FINDING!

What I saw _____

Where I saw it _____

When I saw it _____

Notes _____

_____

_____

ANIMAL SIGHTING OR CLUE FINDING!

What I saw

Where I saw it

When I saw it

Notes

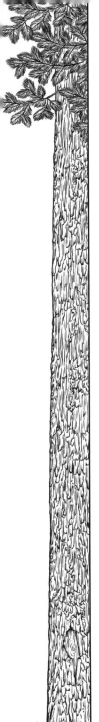

ANIMAL SIGHTING OR CLUE FINDING!

What I saw

Where I saw it

When I saw it

Notes

ANIMAL SIGHTING OR CLUE FINDING!

What I saw _____

Where I saw it _____

When I saw it _____

Notes _____

_____

_____

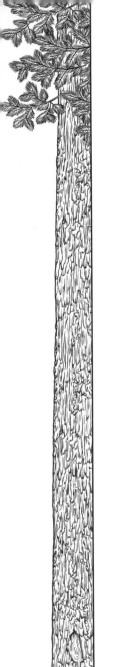

ANIMAL SIGHTING OR CLUE FINDING!

What I saw

Where I saw it

When I saw it

Notes

ANIMAL SIGHTING OR CLUE FINDING!

What I saw

Where I saw it

When I saw it

Notes

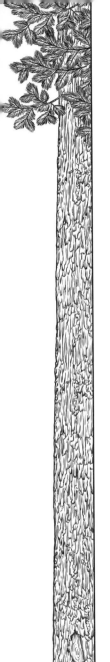

DRAW YOUR FAVORITE ANIMAL

What it is? _____

Where does it live? _____

Notes: _____

_____

Why I like it so much! _____

_____

Who Pooped?

NATURE

Let's get to know more about other living things that you'll find in nature. We'll meet many birds—some that you'll recognize from the *Who Pooped?* series. We'll look at different types of reptiles and amphibians (and stages of metamorphosis). We'll learn about saltwater fish and freshwater fish, and what makes them different. We'll look at different types of insects and arachnids, and why they are not all bugs. And we'll discover common wildflowers and trees in the United States, plus dangerous plants to avoid!

Look for the answers to these creature questions in the next section. See if you got the answers right on page 96.

1. What animal did Benjamin Franklin want as our national symbol?

2. What bird can fly upside down?

3. What reptile can live to be over 100 years old?

4. Which fish can survive out of water as long as it's wet?

5. What creature may have been the first to leave the sea and evolve to live on land?

BIRDS FROM THE *WHO POOPED?* SERIES

☑ Check the birds you have seen on your adventures.

❑ BALD EAGLE

The most famous bird in the United States is the bald eagle—our national symbol since 1782. It is a very large, dark brown bird with a yellow beak, white tail, and a famous white-feathered head. It is a powerful hunter at the top of its food chain.

❑ GREAT HORNED OWL

This owl got its name from the tufts of feathers on its ears that look like horns. It is one of the most common owls in the U.S. and lives in many different environments, from forests and deserts, to swamps and cities. And yes, they HOOT!

❑ NORTHERN FLICKER

This woodpecker is brownish gray with black spots and a patch on its chest, a white behind, and a black or red streak on the sides of its face. It has a long, strong beak for pecking holes in wood to get ants and other insects to eat. It is found throughout the U.S. in forests and woodlands.

❑ COOPER'S HAWK

This medium-sized hawk is mostly blue-gray and brown with dark stripes and a light-colored neck. It is long and lean with a strong, hook-shaped beak. Hawks are found in forests and woodlands across the nation, but you may also see them in your neighborhood.

❑ MALLARD DUCK

Ducks are found all over the world. The most common wild duck in the U.S. is the mallard, and like other ducks, they love the water! The female is primarily brown and white, but the male has gray feathers, a beautiful green head, and a white ring.

❑ WESTERN GREBE

Like ducks, grebes are water birds—in particular, diving birds. Their strong necks and long, thin bills help them spear fish when they dive underwater. They have a black back and cap (the top part of its head), and a white throat and tummy. Babies start riding on their parents' back soon after hatching.

❑ BROWN PELICAN

Pelicans are also diving birds, but they are usually seen on the coasts diving from the air into the water to catch fish with their large bill. The pouch under the bill can hold a lot of fish! They have a white and yellow head and brown body.

❑ WILD TURKEY

Famous for its fanned tail feathers and the male's red head and throat—and Thanksgiving dinner—the turkey is a very large, dark gray-brown bird that you will usually see walking instead of flying. Benjamin Franklin wanted it to be our national symbol instead of the bald eagle.

OTHER COMMON BIRDS IN THE UNITED STATES

> ***DID YOU KNOW:** Most male birds are more colorful than female birds. That's because they need to compete with other males and look good for the girls! Females have duller colors so they don't stand out, which helps hide them from predators when they are nesting.

❏ NORTHERN CARDINAL

A beautiful, bright red bird with feathers making a pointed "crest"on its head and a black mask on its face. It is common in central and eastern states. It is the state bird of more states than any other— seven!

❏ STELLER'S JAY

Crested head, neck, and shoulders are charcoal black, back half of the body is blue with black stripes on wings and tail feathers. It is most often found in western forests.

❏ BLUE JAY

A crested blue, white, and black bird with stripes on its wings and tail feathers, and a black "necklace" (a ring of color that goes around the neck). It is most often found in central and eastern forests.

❏ BELTED KINGFISHER

A crested bird that is grayish blue on the top, white and rust underneath, with a white necklace. Its long, hard beak is shaped to catch fish, and you can find it near water thoughout the U.S.

❏ RAVEN

A large all-black bird with a big, strong beak and "hackles" (bunch of feathers) at its throat. It is found across the U.S.

> **FUN FACT:** Ravens can fly upside down!

❏ RED-WINGED BLACKBIRD

A black bird with yellow-lined red patches on its shoulders. It is commonly found in marshes and wetlands throughout the U.S.

Check the birds you have seen. Color them all!

❑ AMERICAN ROBIN

Found all across the United States, you'll usually see this songbird pulling worms out of the ground. Most of its head and body are dark gray or brown, but it has a bright red-orange chest.

❑ YELLOW-RUMPED WARBLER

During spring, this bird is a beautiful mix of bright yellow, gray, black, and white. During summer, you'll find it in northern and central forests; it flies to the Southeast in winter.

❑ CHIPPING SPARROW

This pretty sparrow has brown and gold wings, a light gray belly and face, a black stripe by each eye, and a reddish-brown "cap" on its head. It is found all across the U.S.

❑ WESTERN MEADOWLARK

It's easy to identify this bird by its bright yellow belly and throat, and the black "V" shape on its chest. You can find it in meadows, grasslands, marshes, fields, and singing on fence posts.

❑ MOURNING DOVE

Gray with black spots on wings, chubby body, and a long pointed tail. It is known for its "cooing" and is found all over the U.S.

❑ DARK-EYED JUNCO

A gray to black, medium-sized sparrow with a white belly, found in western forests and the Appalachian Mountains.

❑ BLACK-CAPPED CHICKADEE

This cute, small, round bird has a black cap and throat that looks like a mask, white cheeks, gray wings and tail, and a tan tummy. You can find it all over the country, usually in trees or shrubs.

❑ RUFOUS HUMMINGBIRD

Males are bright orange with a red throat and females are green. Like other "hummers," it has a long, straight bill good for eating insects and nectar from flowers— and it flies super fast!

TYPES OF REPTILES IN THE UNITED STATES

Reptiles are cold-blooded, air-breathing land animals that have a hard shell or scaly skin. Because they don't have hair like mammals or feathers like birds, their body cannot control its temperature so they move into the sun when they are cold and into the shade when they are too hot. Almost all reptile babies are hatched from eggs.

☑ Check the types of reptiles you have seen.

❏ LIZARDS

Lizards have a long body and tail. They come in many sizes and can have four, two, or no legs. Lizards have been around for almost 200 million years. There are 155 lizard species in North America. A common collared lizard is one species primarily found in southwestern states.

❏ SNAKES

Snakes have a long body covered with scales and no legs. They are carnivores with incredible jaws that open so wide they can eat food bigger than their head! About 50 species of snakes live in the U.S. Some have poisonous venom. The western diamondback rattlesnake is one type of venomous snake.

❏ ALLIGATORS & CROCODILES

Alligators and crocodiles are the largest reptiles, and they look much like giant lizards with a long body and tail, four legs, and scaly skin—except they have a big mouth full of sharp teeth! The differences between "gators" and "crocs" are that alligators have a U-shaped mouth and live in freshwater and crocodiles have a V-shaped mouth and live in saltwater. The American alligator lives in our southeastern states.

❏ TURTLES & TORTOISES

Turtles and tortoises are in the same family and look very similar—both have hard upper and lower shells that surround most of their body for protection. The main difference is that tortoises live on land and turtles spend some time in the water. Turtles have been on earth for more than 200 million years! Some turtles, like the American box turtle, can live a long time, over 100 years!

TYPES OF AMPHIBIANS IN THE UNITED STATES

The word amphibian means "two lives." These creatures begin their lives in the water and then their bodies change, called metamorphosis, to enable them to live on land.

Below is the metamorphosis of an amphibian frog. ☑ Check the stages you have seen. ☑ Then check the types of amphibians you have seen.

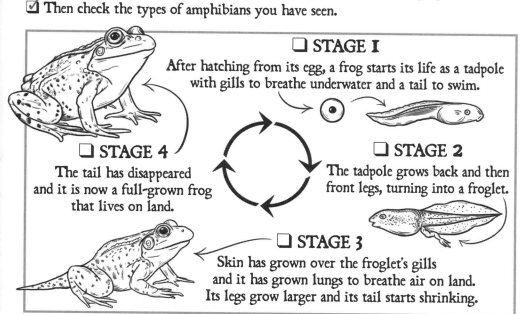

❑ STAGE 1
After hatching from its egg, a frog starts its life as a tadpole with gills to breathe underwater and a tail to swim.

❑ STAGE 2
The tadpole grows back and then front legs, turning into a froglet.

❑ STAGE 3
Skin has grown over the froglet's gills and it has grown lungs to breathe air on land. Its legs grow larger and its tail starts shrinking.

❑ STAGE 4
The tail has disappeared and it is now a full-grown frog that lives on land.

❑ FROGS
Frogs have big eyes, short bodies, powerful long back legs, and webbed fingers and toes. Their skin is smooth and wet with mucus, and they live near water. The American bullfrog is a common frog in the U.S.

❑ SALAMANDERS
Salamanders have long skinny bodies with a long tail and short legs. A newt is a kind of salamander common in the U.S.

❑ TOADS
Toads look a lot like frogs, but they have dry, rough skin, wider bodies, and shorter back legs than frogs. Their skin has a bad taste and smell, so they do not have as many predators as frogs. Toads do not need to live near water.

SALTWATER FISH IN THE UNITED STATES

Fish have been on earth since long before dinosaurs—over 500 millions years! Originally all fish lived in the saltwater of our oceans and seas. Then events like earthquakes and volcanoes moved and re-shaped the earth, and some fish ended up in freshwater locations. This created two main types of fish: saltwater and freshwater. The main difference between them is a big word called osmoregulation, which is how water travels through the fish based on the amount of salt in the water and fish. A saltwater fish has less salt in its body than there is in the water, so water is pulled out of the fish's body and the fish must drink a lot of water to keep from getting dehydrated.

☑ Check the saltwater fish you have seen.

☐ TUNA

Most tuna you eat from a can comes from the Pacific Ocean. Skipjack is the most commonly fished tuna. At around 40 pounds, it is small compared to large tuna like bluefin that can weigh over 1,000 pounds! FUN FACT: tuna can swim super fast at up to 50 miles per hour!

☐ FLOUNDER

Flounder is a flatfish, which means it has a flat, round body. Its coloring is camouflaged to look like the ocean floor, which is where it hangs out while hunting for food. FUN FACT: they have both eyes on one side of their head!

☐ BULL SHARK

Some saltwater fish can live in freshwater. Bull sharks live in the ocean but will swim up rivers in search of food. Unlike most fish, these sharks' kidneys work to pee out more salt when they're in saltwater and retain salt when they're in freshwater. FUN FACT: bull sharks have the strongest bite of all sharks! But don't worry—you are more likely to be hit by lightning than bit by a shark.

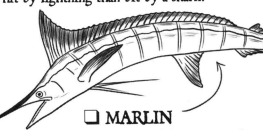

☐ MARLIN

Blue marlin are considered by many to be the most beautiful fish in the world. They are easily recognized by their blue and silver color and the long spear on their nose. FUN FACT: marlin are one of the largest fish in the ocean, weighing in at almost 2,000 pounds!

FRESHWATER FISH IN THE UNITED STATES

Freshwater fish live inland in our lakes, ponds, rivers, and streams. Of approximately 30,000 species of fish, around 40 percent are freshwater fish. These hardy fish had to evolve to adapt to living with less salt in the water. Because their bodies have more salt in them than the fresh water they live in, their bodies take in water through their gills and skin. Unlike saltwater fish, they do not need to drink a lot of water.

☑ Check the freshwater fish you have seen.

❏ AMERICAN EEL

Eels look like snakes but really are fish. Their bodies can be yellow, green, brown, or black, with a light-colored belly. Eels live in both fresh and saltwater. They spawn in the Sargasso Sea in the Atlantic Ocean but spend most of their lives in rivers and streams. FUN FACT: eels can survive out of water for hours as long as they are wet.

❏ TROUT

There are many species of trout. Cutthroat trout are common in western states and a favorite to catch fly-fishing. They can be gold, green, or gray—but all have the red streak across their throat, which is why they got their name "cutthroat." FUN FACT: sea-run cutthroat live in the ocean part of the year.

❏ BASS

Largemouth bass are a favorite among fishermen. You can find them in every state of our country. They are green with a dark stripe and white tummy. FUN FACT: largemouth bass love the color red!

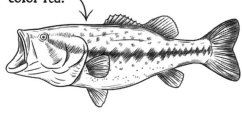

❏ CATFISH

Channel catfish are one of the most popular game fish in the U.S. They are called catfish because they have feelers that look like a cat's whiskers. Catfish come in many colors, from gray, brown, tan or green. FUN FACT: some catfish breathe through their skin!

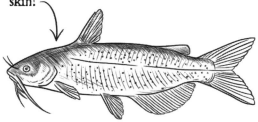

TYPES OF INSECTS IN THE UNITED STATES

There are more than a million species of insects in the world! Insects have antennae, six legs, and are made of three basic parts: the head, thorax, and abdomen. The antennae are attached to the head, and the legs are attached to the thorax. Many people call insects bugs, but true bugs are a type of insect and not all insects are bugs. Most insects have wings, like butterflies. You'll find lots of beautiful butterflies on pages 68 and 69.

☑ Check the types of insects you have seen.

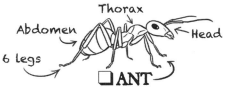

Thorax

Abdomen

Head

6 legs

❏ ANT

Ants live in very large groups called colonies. An ant colony has at least one queen and millions of male ants and female worker ants. Male and queen ants have wings when they are breeding, but female worker ants never have wings. All ants are incredibly strong for their size.

❏ BEE

Bees are known for making honey but are even more important because they pollinate plants by spreading pollen so fruit grows. Many bees have black and yellow stripes.

❏ LADYBUG

Many people think ladybugs are good luck—especially farmers because they eat other insects that damage their crops. Their outer "shell" is actually a set of wings covering another set of wings that they use to fly.

❏ DRAGONFLY

You're most likely to find dragon-flies near water, like a pond or lake, because they hatch from eggs in the water. They also like to eat insects and small fish found in or near water.

❏ TRUE BUG

A true bug has a long special mouth that first pierces, then sucks, the juices from plants or blood from its prey. A cicada is an example of a true bug. (A vampire is not!)

TYPES OF ARACHNIDS IN THE UNITED STATES

Many people think spiders are insects, but they are actually arachnids. Their bodies are made of two basic parts: the head, which is combined with the thorax, and the abdomen. Arachnids have eight legs, but do not have antennae or wings.

☑ Check the types of arachnids you have seen.

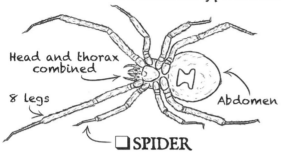

Head and thorax combined

8 legs

Abdomen

❑ SPIDER

Spiders are unique in that they produce silk from spinneret glands in their abdomen. They can make different kinds of silk for different purposes such as a nest for their eggs, a sticky web to catch food, and silk for wrapping their prey in a strong cocoon before injecting them with venom. Most spiders are not dangerous to humans, but there are exceptions like the black widow, which is all black with a red hourglass shape.

❑ TICK

Ticks live in tall grasses, shrubs, and trees. They suck blood from birds and animals, our pets, and people. They are tiny but dangerous because they can carry serious diseases, so make sure you wear a long-sleeved shirt and long pants tucked into socks with shoes when out hiking or playing where ticks live. And have an adult help you check for ticks afterwards.

❑ SCORPION

A scorpion has eight legs like other arachnids, but it also has two pincers (claws) that it uses to grab its prey, and a tail with a poisonous end that curves up over its back ready to sting its prey or predator. Its venom is strong enough to kill small prey, but only a few have venom strong enough to kill a human. They live in deserts, grasslands, and caves, and burrow under rocks into soil to hide.

FUN FACT: scorpions look like lobsters and have been around since before dinosaurs, hundreds of millions of years ago. Many scientists think they may have been the first creatures to come out of the sea and evolve to live on land.

COMMON BUTTERFLIES IN THE UNITED STATES

Butterflies are considered by many to be the most beautiful of the flying insects!
Below is the lifecycle of a butterfly. ☑ Check the stages you have seen.

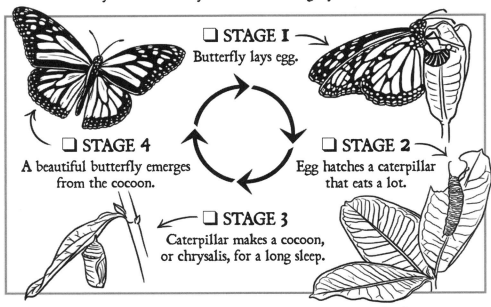

❏ **STAGE 1**
Butterfly lays egg.

❏ **STAGE 2**
Egg hatches a caterpillar
that eats a lot.

❏ **STAGE 3**
Caterpillar makes a cocoon,
or chrysalis, for a long sleep.

❏ **STAGE 4**
A beautiful butterfly emerges
from the cocoon.

❏ TIGER SWALLOWTAILS

A large, bright yellow and black "tiger-
striped" butterfly with long, thin extensions
on the hind wings called swallowtails.

❏ BLACK SWALLOWTAILS

A black butterfly with two rows of yellow
spots, blue between the rows on the hind wings, as
well as a bright red spot with a black center dot.

❏ CABBAGE WHITE

A common small, white butterfly
with black-tipped forewings and
black dots.

☑ Check the common butterflies you have seen. Color them all!

❏ ORANGE SULPHUR

A small to medium sized, yellow to orange butterfly with black-tipped forewings and black dots.

❏ MONARCH

With bright orange and black wings with white spots, the monarch is one of the most beautiful and well-known butterflies in the U.S.

❏ MOURNING CLOAK

A large, dark purple to dark brown butterfly with yellow-edged wings and a row of blue dots.

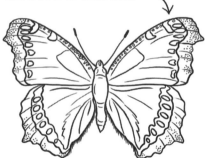

❏ SPRING AZURE

This small, bright blue butterfly is one of the first butterflies to emerge from its cocoon in spring.

❏ GRAY HAIRSTREAK

A common small, gray butterfly with an orange spot on each hind wing.

❏ QUESTION MARK

The underside of this orange to red butterfly's hind wings has a white shape that looks like a question mark.

COMMON WILDFLOWERS IN THE UNITED STATES

*IMPORTANT: do not eat any plants you find in the wild. What looks like an edible plant may actually be poisonous! ☑ Check the wildflowers you have seen.

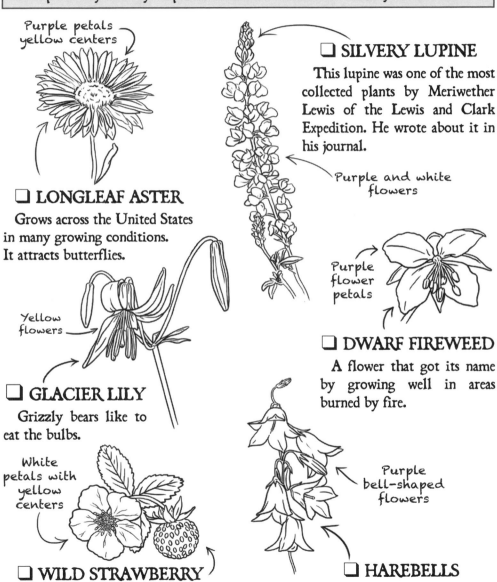

Purple petals yellow centers

❑ **LONGLEAF ASTER**

Grows across the United States in many growing conditions. It attracts butterflies.

Yellow flowers

❑ **GLACIER LILY**

Grizzly bears like to eat the bulbs.

White petals with yellow centers

❑ **WILD STRAWBERRY**

Grows red berries, delicious cousin to supermarket strawberries.

❑ **SILVERY LUPINE**

This lupine was one of the most collected plants by Meriwether Lewis of the Lewis and Clark Expedition. He wrote about it in his journal.

Purple and white flowers

Purple flower petals

❑ **DWARF FIREWEED**

A flower that got its name by growing well in areas burned by fire.

Purple bell-shaped flowers

❑ **HAREBELLS**

Delicate stems can have one or several flowers.

MOUNTAIN BLUEBELLS

Flowers are eaten by animals, especially goats and sheep. Native Americans made a tea with it for medicine.

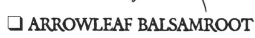

Clusters of small blue flowers

Brownish-purple flower petals

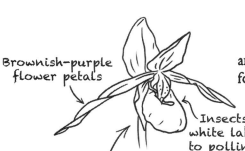

Insects land on the white labellum (pouch) to pollinate the flower

MOUNTAIN LADY'S SLIPPER

These orchids are somewhat rare and are protected by law in some states.

Bright pink to white petals

Yellow

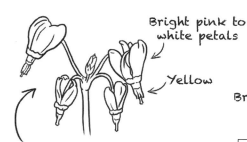

Bright yellow flowers

SHOOTING STAR

Flowers come to a yellow point resembling shooting stars.

ARROWLEAF BALSAMROOT

Native Americans used all parts of the plant for food and medicine.

Orange spotted flowers

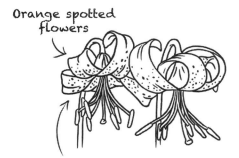

Bright red flowers that look like a paintbrush dipped in red paint

PAINTBRUSH

This plant was used by Native Americans as both a love charm and a poison. Do not eat!

LEOPARD LILY

The bulbs were eaten by Native Americans. Large and small animals also enjoy eating them.

COMMON TREES IN THE UNITED STATES

Identify a tree by its leaves, needles, and cones. ☑ Check the trees you have seen.

❏ RED MAPLE

A favorite for its brillant color, it's the most common tree across the U.S. Red maple has something red for every season: red buds in winter, red flowers in spring, red leaf stalks in summer, and red leaves in autumn.

❏ AMERICAN SWEETGUM

Most often found in southeastern states, the sweetgum is a deciduous tree, meaning it drops its colorful leaves in the fall and regrows new leaves in the spring. **FUN FACT:** its resin is used to make chewing gum and medicine!

❏ LOBLOLLY PINE

Unlike other pine trees that grow in dry soil in cold areas of the country, the fast-growing loblolly pine grows well in wet soil where it's hot, typically in southern and coastal states.

❏ QUAKING ASPEN

Named "quaking" because its leaves shake with even a small breeze, this deciduous tree sparkles in the fall when sunlight hits its bright yellow leaves. It grows in more diverse habitats than any other tree in the U.S.

❏ DOUGLAS-FIR

This evergreen is one of our most loved trees—popular for lumber and as a Christmas tree!

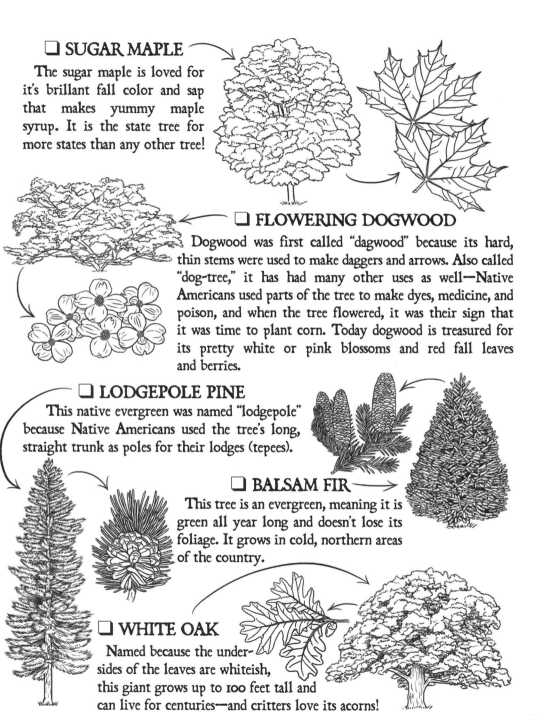

❏ SUGAR MAPLE

The sugar maple is loved for it's brillant fall color and sap that makes yummy maple syrup. It is the state tree for more states than any other tree!

❏ FLOWERING DOGWOOD

Dogwood was first called "dagwood" because its hard, thin stems were used to make daggers and arrows. Also called "dog-tree," it has had many other uses as well—Native Americans used parts of the tree to make dyes, medicine, and poison, and when the tree flowered, it was their sign that it was time to plant corn. Today dogwood is treasured for its pretty white or pink blossoms and red fall leaves and berries.

❏ LODGEPOLE PINE

This native evergreen was named "lodgepole" because Native Americans used the tree's long, straight trunk as poles for their lodges (tepees).

❏ BALSAM FIR

This tree is an evergreen, meaning it is green all year long and doesn't lose its foliage. It grows in cold, northern areas of the country.

❏ WHITE OAK

Named because the under-sides of the leaves are whiteish, this giant grows up to 100 feet tall and can live for centuries—and critters love its acorns!

POISONOUS PLANTS TO AVOID!

These plants can give you a rash that is itchy and hurts, so it's best to avoid them. The first step is to identify them. All have multiple leaflets that make up the main leaves, called compound leaves. While some fall under the old rule "leaves of three, leave it be," not all have three—and there are many safe plants that also have three leaflets. Another clue is that these toxic plants have a waxy look from the oily poison called urushiol. If you will be playing in an area that might have these plants, be sure to wear long sleeves and long pants tucked into socks. Wash any clothing that comes in contact with these plants.

☑ Check the dangerous plants you have seen.

❏ POISON IVY

Poison ivy grows in almost every state in the country. It usually has three pointed leaflets per compound leaf, yellowish flowers, and white berries. The center leaf is larger and has a stem. New leaves can be reddish, and in fall leaves turn yellow to red. Poison ivy can grow as a vine or shrub.

❏ POISON OAK

Poison oak is found in the West Coast and southeastern states. It can grow as a shrub or a vine. It usually has three leaflets that look like oak leaves, but can have more. Leaves can be green or red and have yellowish flowers or light green berries.

❏ POISON SUMAC

Poison sumac has a double row of leaflets with one on the end. It breaks the three leaflets rule, having seven to thirteen leaflets on a red stem. These tall shrubs or small trees like wet environments like swamps and bogs.

TREATMENT

If you touch one of these plants, gently wash the area immediately with soap and water. If you get an itchy, blistery rash, apply a cool wet cloth and calamine lotion—and try hard not to scratch it! It's also a good idea to see your doctor, especially if you have a large rash, fever, or other severe reaction.

Who Pooped?
MY NATURE FIELD JOURNAL

Keeping a nature field journal helps us observe the great outdoors, and appreciate how incredible and beautiful our planet is! This is the place to record your experiences with nature: what you see, what you hear, what you smell, and what you feel. Use all your senses and be creative!

Ideas for your nature field journal include:

- Drawings or photos of critters, plants, or landscapes.
- Tape in flowers, leaves, or feathers (but not from national parks!).
- Write field notes. Describe the scent of a flower, the colors of a butterfly, the sounds you heard, what season it was, what colors the leaves were, the texture of a tree trunk or rock, or note something you've never seen before and want to research later.
- Make a leaf rubbing by putting a leaf under the page and coloring a solid color over it with a pencil or crayon.
- Make a leaf or rock stamp by painting on one side, then pressing the paint side down onto the paper like a stamp. Carefully lift the leaf or rock and let the paint dry thoroughly before closing the page.
- Make a quick sketch in pencil of something you want to finish with color and more detail once you get home.

Remember—there is no right or wrong way to journal because it's yours! Do what you want.

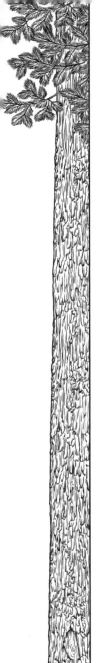

THINGS I OBSERVED IN NATURE

What I saw _____

Where I saw it _____

When I saw it _____

Details _____

_____

_____

THINGS I OBSERVED IN NATURE

What I saw _____

Where I saw it _____

When I saw it _____

Details _____

_____

_____

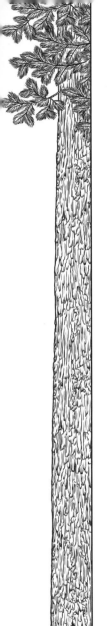

THINGS I OBSERVED IN NATURE

What I saw _____

Where I saw it _____

When I saw it _____

Details _____

_____

_____

THINGS I OBSERVED IN NATURE

What I saw _____

Where I saw it _____

When I saw it _____

Details _____

_____

_____

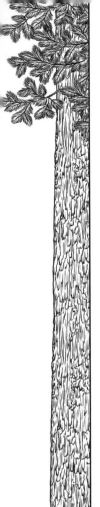

SCAVENGER HUNT

Check, note, and draw the items you found on your nature adventures.

☐ Track	☐ Scat	☐ Bird	☐ Insect
☐ Pinecone	☐ Wildflower	☐ Leaf	☐ Large Animal
☐ Small Animal	☐ Fish	☐ Feather	☐ Amphibian
☐ Smooth Rock	☐ Arachnid	☐ Reptile	☐ Butterfly

Who Pooped?™

THE SKY

Look up into the sky. What do you see? If it is night and you are away from city lights and don't have a lot of clouds, you probably see many stars. Do you see any patterns that look like an animal, a person, a strange creature, or an object? Patterns of stars are called constellations, and many have stories passed down since ancient Greek times, originally recorded by the Greek astronomer Ptolemy. In ancient times, people followed the constellations like a calendar in the sky to know when to plant and harvest crops, and as a map for traveling on land and sea.

There are eighty-eight different constellations: forty-eight ancient Greek constellations and forty newer constellations. Star maps use the brightest stars to make up the constellations, as we see them from Earth. The brightest stars are so bright because they are either closest to us, the largest, or double stars. You won't be able to see all the constellations from one point on Earth, like your backyard—their visibility depends on where you are and the season— and they cover the entire sky that goes around our planet! So let's look at a few that you are most likely to see in the United States. Connect the stars that make up the constellations and ☑ check the boxes of those you've seen. After that, we'll discover some neat facts about the Moon, Sun, and clouds!

FUN FACTS

- Some constellations are grouped together by stories from Greek mythology. The groups are sometimes called a family. The Orion family consists of four constellations: the great hunter Orion, his two hunting dogs, and the hare that they chase across the night sky.

- There can be many different versions of the stories about constellatons because they have been told and retold over many generations by people living in many different regions. Different versions of the stories can include different constellations in the family. For example, some versions of the Orion family story have a scorpion that chases Orion, and some have Orion battling Taurus, the bull.

❑ CANIS MINOR, the Small Dog

Like their master, Orion's two hunting dogs, Canis Minor and Canis Major, can best be seen in the southwest sky in winter. Like many constellations, the star map doesn't look much like what it represents, in this case a small dog. Canis Minor is usually just shown as two stars.

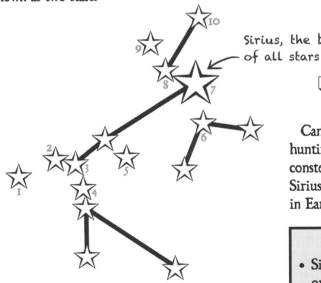

Sirius, the brightest
of all stars

❑ CANIS MAJOR, the Great Dog

Canis Major is Orion's large hunting dog. What makes this constellation so special is its star Sirius, which is the brightest star in Earth's sky.

FUN FACTS

- Sirius is actually a double— or binary—star.

- Sirius is sometimes called "Dog Star."

❑ ORION, the Hunter

Orion is one of the most popular constellations because it is very bright and can be seen from most places around the world. In the United States, it is best seen in the southwest sky in winter. It is named after the hunter Orion from Greek mythology, who was the son of the sea god Poseidon. Some stories say he carries a big bronze club that is unbreakable, and a bow. Can you see them in the constellation?

The easiest way to find Orion in the sky is to look for the three bright stars that make up his belt.

CONCERNING FACT

- Light pollution is when there is too much artificial light from cities and towns. Not only does it make it much harder to see stars, it also has a negative effect on wildlife and people. Some parks, called Dark Sky Parks, have stargazing areas with minimal artificial light.

❑ LEPUS, the Hare

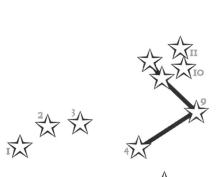

Lepus is right under Orion's feet. Stories from Greek mythology say that Orion and his two dogs are forever chasing the hare across the night sky. Lepus has a long tail and two tall ears. Can you see them?

❑ URSA MINOR, Little Bear

Ursa Minor is named after a small bear. It is also called the Little Dipper, famous because at the end of its handle, which is also the bear's long tail, is its brightest star, Polaris, also called the North Star. Positioned over the North Pole, the North Star has guided people by land and sea since ancient times.

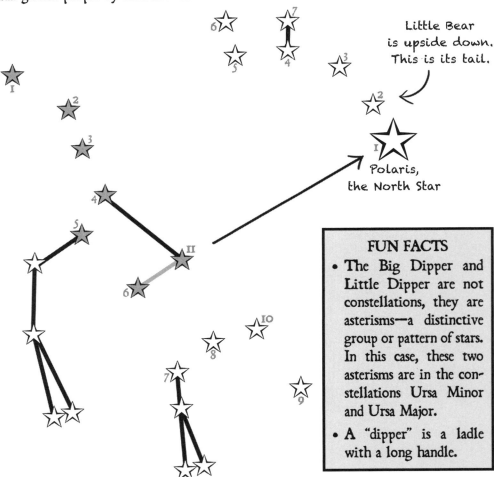

Little Bear is upside down. This is its tail.

Polaris, the North Star

FUN FACTS

- The Big Dipper and Little Dipper are not constellations, they are asterisms—a distinctive group or pattern of stars. In this case, these two asterisms are in the constellations Ursa Minor and Ursa Major.

- A "dipper" is a ladle with a long handle.

❑ URSA MAJOR, the Great Bear

Ursa Major is the largest constellation in the northern sky and can be seen all over the United States. Its brightest stars (shown in gray) make up the Big Dipper, which is one of the most recognizable star patterns in the sky—very important because it is easily seen and it points to the North Star.

IF I MADE MY OWN CONSTELLATION
IT WOULD LOOK LIKE THIS

What it looks like _____

Story about my constellation _____

_____

_____

_____

MOON PHASES

While it looks like the Moon changes shape, it is really always round. What we see is the lit part of the Moon that is reflecting light from the Sun. The other part is dark so we can't see it. The sun always lights up half the Moon, like it lights up half the Earth, making our day and night. So why don't we always see half a moon? Because as the Moon orbits the Earth, we see the lit part from different angles, making it look like the Moon is different shapes. These are the Moon phases and there are eight.

Look into the night sky and ☑ check the Moon phases you see at the bottom of the page.

The Sun lights up the half of the Moon and Earth facing it.

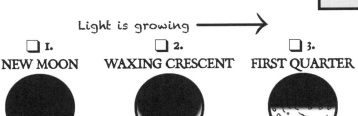

Night

Day

EARTH

Moon Orbit

SUN

FUN FACTS
- The Moon phases repeat every 29.5 days.
- A lunar eclipse is when the Sun, Earth, and Moon align and the Moon is in the Earth's shadow.
- Earth's moon is the 5th largest in the solar system.

WHAT'S IT MEAN?
- **WAXING** means the light is growing.
- **WANING** means the light is shrinking.
- **GIBBOUS** means the moon is over half lit.
- **CRESCENT** means only a curved sliver shows.

Light is growing ⟶

☐ 1.
NEW MOON

☐ 2.
WAXING CRESCENT

☐ 3.
FIRST QUARTER

☐ 4.
WAXING GIBBOUS

Color in the moons below to show the eight phases of the Moon. As you can see from the bottom of the page, with each phase the light first grows and then shrinks as the Moon orbits the Earth.

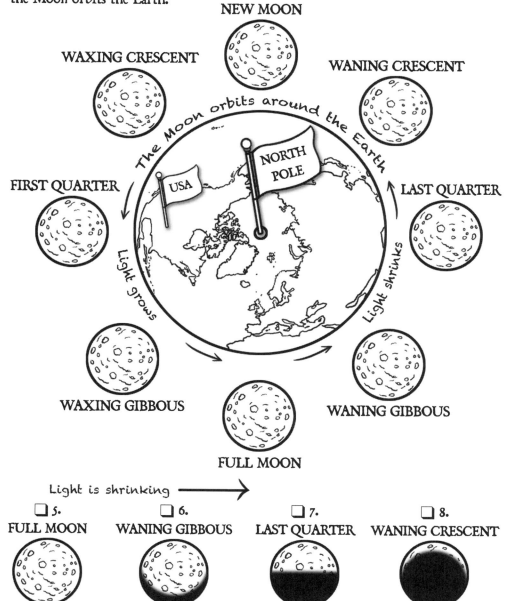

NEW MOON

WAXING CRESCENT

WANING CRESCENT

The Moon orbits around the Earth

FIRST QUARTER

USA

NORTH POLE

LAST QUARTER

Light grows

Light shrinks

WAXING GIBBOUS

WANING GIBBOUS

FULL MOON

Light is shrinking ⟶

☐ 5.
FULL MOON

☐ 6.
WANING GIBBOUS

☐ 7.
LAST QUARTER

☐ 8.
WANING CRESCENT

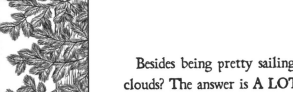

CLOUDS

Besides being pretty sailing overhead in shapes like animals, what's so great about clouds? The answer is **A LOT!** They bring much-needed rain for all living creatures and plants to survive, they help control the temperatures on Earth, and they can help us predict what weather is coming so we can be prepared.

Clouds are created when warm air from the ground rises and then cools. All of our air holds moisture called water vapor, but warm air can hold more, so when it rises and cools, the vapor turns into tiny water drops or ice crystals that gather together, float, and create clouds. When clouds look white, they are reflecting sunlight. When they look gray, they have too much water in them to reflect light.

There are four main types of clouds: cirrus, cumulus, stratus, and nimbus. ☑ Check the clouds you have seen.

❑ CUMULUS

Cumulus clouds are pretty, puffy clouds that look like cotton. If they are close to the ground, white, and not very tall, it means good weather. If they grow tall and dark, they turn into cumulonimbus, often called thunderheads, and then you know heavy rain, hail, or even dangerous tornados can be coming!

❑ STRATUS

Stratus clouds are lower in the sky and flatter, and they look like a puffy blanket that covers the sky. They can be hiding other clouds above them. These clouds are overhead on cloudy, light rainy, or snowy days.

FUN FACTS
- Fog is stratus clouds that form on the ground.
- Greenish clouds can mean a tornado is coming.
- Cirrus clouds can travel really fast—up to 100 miles per hour!

Puffy, white clouds

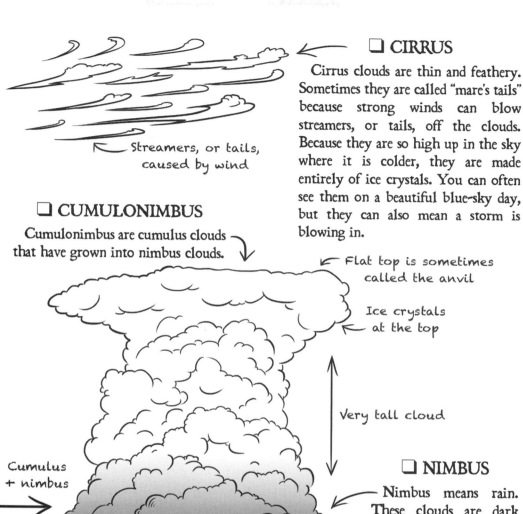

Streamers, or tails,
caused by wind

❑ CIRRUS

Cirrus clouds are thin and feathery. Sometimes they are called "mare's tails" because strong winds can blow streamers, or tails, off the clouds. Because they are so high up in the sky where it is colder, they are made entirely of ice crystals. You can often see them on a beautiful blue-sky day, but they can also mean a storm is blowing in.

❑ CUMULONIMBUS

Cumulonimbus are cumulus clouds that have grown into nimbus clouds.

Flat top is sometimes called the anvil

Ice crystals at the top

Very tall cloud

Cumulus + nimbus

❑ NIMBUS

Nimbus means rain. These clouds are dark because they are holding a lot of water, so they are seen when there is a rain or snow storm. They often bring thunder and lightning. Stratus and cumulus clouds can also turn into nimbus clouds.

These clouds look very dark from the ground because they are heavy with water drops at the bottom.

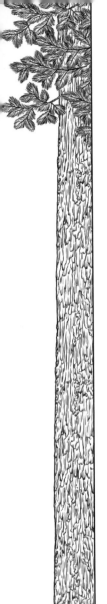

CLOUD SPOTTING

Have you ever looked up at the clouds and they look like an animal or other shape? That's called cloud spotting and it's fun! So go out on a beautiful day, find a comfortable place to sit or lie down, look up at the clouds, and let your imagination go to work finding shapes. In the box below, draw a cloud shape that you've seen. You can even make up a story about it. Remember—you can "tip-in" more pages if you want!

Cloud shape _____

Where I saw it _____

When I saw it _____

Cloud story _____

_____

_____

_____

BOOKS I'VE READ

After you've read a book from the *Who Pooped?* series, color in your official badge. After you've earned all the *Who Pooped?* badges, fill in your official *Who Pooped?* Certificate of Completion.

Who Pooped? GRAND TETON NATIONAL PARK

Who Pooped? GREAT SMOKY MOUNTAINS NATIONAL PARK

Who Pooped? NORTHWOODS

Who Pooped? OLYMPIC

Who Pooped? RED ROCK CANYON

Who Pooped? REDWOODS